CURSED TOMBS AND LOST TREASURE

INVESTIGATING HISTORY'S MYSTERIES

Louise Spilsbury

CHERITON
CHILDREN'S BOOKS

Published in 2024 by **Cheriton Children's Books**
1 Bank Drive West, Shrewsbury, Shropshire, SY3 9DJ, UK

© 2024 Cheriton Children's Books

First Edition

Author: Louise Spilsbury
Designer: Jessica Moon
Editor: Jennifer Sanderson
Proofreader: Katie Dicker

Picture credits: Cover: Shutterstock/Kiselev Andrey Valerevich (fg), Shutterstock/Melnikov Dmitriy (bg). Inside: p1: Shutterstock/319photo, p4: Shutterstock/Tunatura, p5: Shutterstock/Levent Konuk, p7b: Shutterstock/FXQuadro, p7t: Shutterstock/Potifor, p9b: Shutterstock/Byjeng, p9t: Shutterstock/John Theodor, p10: Shutterstock/papi8888, p11: Shutterstock/Everett Collection, p12: Shutterstock/Melnikov Dmitriy, p13: Shutterstock/Kiselev Andrey Valerevich, p14b: Shutterstock/Denis S, p14t: Shutterstock/Declan Hillman, p16: Shutterstock/Andrea Izzotti, p17: Wikimedia Commons/Flickr/Aidan McRae Thomson, p18: Shutterstock/Prachaya Roekdeethaweesab, p19: Shutterstock/Jaroslav Moravcik, p20l: Shutterstock/Almazoff, p20r: Shutterstock/Vagengeim, p21: Shutterstock/Jono Photography, p22: Shutterstock/Maksim Gulyachik, p23: Shutterstock/IG Digital Arts, p25b: Shutterstock/raymoe81, p25t: Shutterstock/319photo, p26bl: Shutterstock/jdross75, p26br: Shutterstock/Tetris Awakening, p27: Shutterstock/Vladimir Korostyshevskiy, p28: Wikimedia Commons/ProtoplasmaKid, p29: Shutterstock/Michael Dechev, p30: Shutterstock/Eskystudio, p31: Shutterstock/El Coco Velazquez, p33b: Shutterstock/FXQuadro, p33t: Shutterstock/Kichigin, p35b: Shutterstock/Artem Mazunov, p35t: Shutterstock/Kyuandzo, p36: Wikimedia Commons/Francis_Sartorius/Royal Museums Greenwich, p37bl: Shutterstock/Unterwegs, p37br: Shutterstock/thisdesign, p38: Shutterstock/3Dsculptor, p39: Shutterstock/Netfalls Remy Musser, p41b: Shutterstock/Fer Gregory, p41t: Shutterstock/Dinar Omarov, p42: Shutterstock/Fahroni, p45: Shutterstock/Luis Louro.

All rights reserved. No part of this book may be reproduced in any form without permission from the publisher, except by a reviewer.

Printed in China

Please visit our website,
www.cheritonchildrensbooks.com
to see more of our high-quality books.

CONTENTS

Chapter 1 Treasure Seekers 4
   Investigating Timur's Tomb 10

Chapter 2 Cruel and Cursed 12
   Investigating King Tut's Tomb 18

Chapter 3 Deadly Tombs 20
   Investigating Qin's Burial Site 24

Chapter 4 Treasure-Filled Tombs 26
   Investigating Missing Inca Gold 32

Chapter 5 Swallowed by the Sea 34
   Investigating a Slave Ship 38

Chapter 6 Treasure Hunters in Action 40
   Investigating the Knights 44

Glossary 46
Find Out More 47
Index and About the Author 48

CHAPTER 1

TREASURE SEEKERS

What does it take to be a treasure hunter? To brave the difficult journeys to remote, or faraway, deserts where no one else ventures, or the deep, dark seas in search of wealth or historical riches? Perhaps it means becoming a victim of a scary and deadly curse that is said to protect some ancient **burial sites** from being opened and robbed? People have been fascinated, and scared, by tales of lost treasure and cursed tombs for centuries. Some of those who set off to find these fabled fortunes are never seen again.

Secret Stashes

Some treasure is buried on purpose. Long ago, there were no banks, so people buried and hid their money and gold for safekeeping. Sometimes, people forgot where they left their stashes or they left their homes in a hurry because of war or disaster, so didn't have time to get them. Pirates may have buried treasure in secret locations so they could escape being caught. They may have made a map to locate it, but then died at sea before they could return to claim it.

Scary Curses

In some **cultures**, gold, gems, and other riches were buried with important people in their tombs. They believed those people could use the riches in another life after death that is known as the afterlife. Sometimes, people painted curses threatening painful deaths on the tomb walls. People told stories of these dreadful curses to keep others away from the terrifying tombs.

Do hoards of wealth lie hidden in tombs, guarded by the dead buried there?

Lost in Time

A lot of treasure was simply lost in time. In the past, mighty ships crisscrossed the oceans, filled with valuable goods to trade with other countries. These ships were often wrecked by storms or attacked by pirates or enemies. The ships sank to the ocean floor with their treasure hidden inside them, too deep and difficult to collect. Sometimes, there are records of such shipwrecks, and treasure hunters may use these clues to try and find the hidden riches.

How much treasure lies at the bottom of the ocean?

SET TO SPOOK!

In this book, we are going to explore some of the most intriguing and creepy reports of cursed tombs and buried treasure. You'll hear about doomed treasure hunters, golden death masks, and riches discovered after hundreds of years. Some of the stories will send shivers down your spine. Some of them will leave you truly spooked!

Lost City of Gold?

Imagine a city of pure, dazzling gold, lighting up the trees and hills all around it. The idea of the lost city of El Dorado lured many treasure hunters to their deaths. They heard **legends** of a solid-gold city that was bursting with treasures, hidden deep in the South American jungle. In the sixteenth and seventeenth centuries, early groups of Spanish and then other European explorers traveled into the dense, damp rain forests and high, challenging mountains in this area in search of unimaginable wealth. Many people lost their lives along the way or vanished without a trace.

Fact or Fiction?

Today, the evidence, or proof, suggests that El Dorado was not a city at all but, instead, a person. Legend tells of an ancient king who covered himself in gold dust from head to toe during festivals, then dove from a raft into Lake Guatavita in Colombia. The lake was thought to be **sacred**. Some people say that there could still be treasure in Lake Guatavita because they believe ancient people tossed gold into the water as offerings to their goddess of water.

The El Dorado of the North

When French explorers landed in present-day Canada in the 1500s, they heard a legend of a kingdom said to be full of gold, rubies, and other treasures. The French called it the Kingdom of Saguenay. This kingdom was supposed to be full of blond-haired people with endless riches, and was located somewhere along the shores north of the Saint Lawrence River in Quebec. It became known as the El Dorado of the North.

Fools' Gold?

The French government sent ships to hunt for the treasure and the great mines of silver and gold they had heard about. Explorers sent back what they thought were diamonds and gold, but they turned out to be worthless quartz crystals and iron pyrites, which are a type of rock also known as fool's gold. For years, explorers searched for the Kingdom of Saguenay in vain. Perhaps it never existed and was just a myth, or a made-up story? Or perhaps the local Iroquoian people whose land the French took told them the story to trick or confuse them.

SPOOKED!

Some people say Saguenay could have been a place where early **Norse** settlers arrived in Newfoundland, Canada, centuries before. Could the blond-haired people in the Iroquoian legend be Vikings who left some of their stolen treasures behind?

Did the Vikings settle near the Saint Lawrence River and then leave their riches there? Early explorers never found the Kingdom of Saguenay. Did it ever exist, and if so, where is it now?

The Bad King's Lost Treasure

There's an area in Norfolk, United Kingdom (UK), which is known as the Wash. In places, this **marsh** is a very dangerous area of mud, **quicksand**, and hidden streams. It has swallowed up many an unlucky walker and even a king's treasure hoard, if legends are to be believed.

John the Bad

King John of England ruled from 1199 to 1216. He was known as "Bad King John" because he was **tyrannous**, cowardly, and cruel. He took huge amounts of money from his people and used it to collect jewelry and gold plates, among other treasures.

Swallowed by Mud

In 1216, King John was on the run from one of his many enemies. With him was a group of more than 2,000 people and a baggage train, which contained the king's prized possessions. The train was made up of wagons and was more than 1 mile (1.6 km) long. The story goes that as the group tried to cross the dangerous Wash, the rising waters swept away the wagons and their precious contents. The king died a week later, taking the secret of exactly what treasure was in the missing hoard with him to his grave.

A Real Treasure Map?

Archeologists are people who look for artifacts, or items from the past, to try to understand ancient ways of life. In 1952, archeologists working in caves overlooking the northern end of the Dead Sea in Palestine in the Middle East, discovered two thin, rolled-up sheets of copper. When they figured out the ancient writing on the scrolls, they were amazed. It turned out to be a detailed list of more than 60 places where large amounts of gold and silver were supposedly hidden. However, there was to be a twist in the tale...

Secrets in the Scrolls

The problem was that the instructions on the scrolls are impossible to follow. The locations written on the scrolls don't include precise instructions and some of the words used are unknown to us. They also mention places that no longer exist. The scrolls are probably 2,000 years old, so there is also a chance that people have already found and taken the lost treasure. Some people say that the copper scrolls are a hoax, or prank, and there is no lost treasure waiting to be found. But, what if some of the treasure is still out there, even after all these years?

SPOOKED!

Some people believe that Romans who invaded the area around present-day Palestine would have found all of the treasure because the Romans had a nasty habit of torturing, or hurting, people to make them reveal the location of their secret stashes.

The locations of the hidden treasure in the copper scrolls remains a secret.

INVESTIGATING TIMUR'S TOMB

Spooky Curses

Samarkand, which is now part of Uzbekistan, was part of the **Soviet Union**. In 1941, worried chatter filled its streets: "The Russian **expedition** is going to open the tomb of Timur the Great! It will bring the curse on our heads!" Timur was one of the most ruthless, or cruel, invaders in history, and local people feared that opening his coffin would bring untold horrors. Their worst fear had come true.

Timur's Reign of Terror

Timur controlled a huge part of Asia during the fourteenth century. He was a skilled military leader whose armies are said to have killed millions of people. Timur even ordered the building of a pyramid of 70,000 human skulls in Iran. In 1941, the Soviet leader Josef Stalin sent a team of archeologists to open a tomb in Samarkand to find out if it was Timur's and his closest relatives. This was against the wishes of the people who lived there and their religious leaders.

The Curse of Timur's Tomb

When the Russian archeologists opened the coffin, it is said they found a dreadful curse written inside it that gave a terrifying warning: "Whoever opens my tomb shall unleash an invader more terrible than I."

Timur is said to have punished enemies who refused to surrender by killing them and building a pyramid with their heads.

Did Timur's curse bring bad luck to the Russians and lead to the invasion of their country?

Unleashing a Curse

When Timur's tomb was opened, and the remains inside removed, the room was filled with a sharp, unpleasant smell that made the archeologists choke. This was thought to be from the mixture of oils, scents, and other substances used to preserve, or embalm, Timur's body. Timur had died on his way to China and his body had been treated to preserve it for the long journey back to his hometown. Some people said that the smell was the sign that opening the tomb unleashed dreadful curses.

Timur's Terrible Threat

Two days after the opening of the tomb, the Germans under Adolf Hitler's leadership invaded the Soviet Union. Many people linked the invasion with the opening of the tomb of Timur. Millions of people died as a result of the invasion. In 1942, Stalin ordered Timur's remains to be taken back to Samarkand and reburied following the proper religious **rituals**. Shortly after this, the German Army retreated from the Soviet Union.

CHAPTER 2

CRUEL AND CURSED

It is all too easy to imagine getting lost in the spooky maze of dark tunnels deep inside an ancient Egyptian pyramid. There are confusing passageways, sliding doors, hidden doorways, secret chambers, and trapdoors. Some pyramids have bridges and ramps that lead to dead ends. If those who dare to enter panic and become lost, they could be trapped deep within the pyramid walls, never to be seen again.

Treasures in the Tombs

The pharaohs were the mighty rulers of ancient Egypt, a great civilization that was at its height around 3,000 years ago. When the pharaohs died, they were buried in the darkest, deepest depths of a pyramid. The ancient Egyptians believed that there was a life after death, so they buried their dead with all the goods they thought they would need in the afterlife.

Buried with Riches

When the pharaohs were alive, they decorated themselves with gold, jewels, and perfumes, so they took these treasures with them to their graves. To help protect the pharaoh and their treasures, walls of the inner tomb were painted with spells. The Egyptians believed these helped people pass safely into the afterlife.

Would you dare to go deep inside an ancient pharaoh's tomb?

Some curses say that when Egyptian tombs are opened, the mummy inside comes to life and chases and murders the grave robbers!

Making Mummies

Before a pharaoh was buried, their body was mummified. This procedure preserved the body so that the pharaoh would be able to use it in the afterlife. Some Egyptian mummies were buried in two or three different coffins, one inside another. The outer stone coffin was called a sarcophagus. The coffin was richly decorated, and sometimes made from gold.

The Curse of the Pharaohs

Anyone who disturbs a pharaoh's tomb or a mummy risks facing the curse of the pharaohs. This legendary curse is believed to cause death, illness, or bad luck. In fact, most people believe that the idea of a curse was created to stop people robbing the pyramids. Some say it could be real. But actually, people could simply die from diseases caused by the **bacteria** or **fungi** found on the ancient treasures.

SPOOKED!

Preparing mummies must have been a creepy and smelly job! After cleaning the body, parts such as the liver and stomach were removed. The heart was left inside. The body was covered in powder for 40 days to dry it out. Then the skin was oiled to stop it cracking. Rags and straw were stuffed inside to give it a lifelike shape. Finally, the body was wrapped in bandages to help preserve it.

Could Cleopatra's tomb lie beneath the waves?

This is the amazing silver coffin of Shoshenq II, with its incredible hawk head.

The Treasures of Tanis

Most royal Egyptian tombs were broken into and robbed by thieves long ago. But in 1939, an archeologist named Pierre Montet discovered the Treasures of Tanis. He found an entire **complex** of royal burial places, including unopened pharaohs' tombs filled with gold and silver treasures. Among the treasures were gold masks, solid silver coffins, and spectacular gold and silver jewelry. The rich treasures are one of the greatest archeological discoveries of all time.

A Hawk-Headed Silver Coffin

The 1939 finds included a hawk-headed solid silver coffin belonging to Shoshenq II, who was until then an unknown king. In ancient Egypt, people believed the hawk had protective powers and the bird was linked to royalty. Hawks were rulers of the skies, protecting Earth with their wings. Inside one of the silver coffins at Tanis was a pharaoh named Psusennes. His body was covered with a gold mask, 6 gold and **lapis-lazuli** necklaces, 26 bracelets, and 2 chest plates. The larger necklace weighed almost 18 pounds (8 kg) and it was made of thousands of separate pieces of gold.

INVESTIGATING KING TUT'S TOMB

Spooky Circumstances

When British archeologist Howard Carter and his team discovered the tomb of the pharaoh Tutankhamun in 1922, they found a coffin of solid gold, a beautiful throne, and countless other incredible treasures. The team celebrated its remarkable finds. But, within 8 years of opening the tomb, some people connected with the discovery were dead, some in mysterious circumstances. Were they all victims of the Curse of the Pharaohs?

A Day of Doom?

Rumors started to spread that the tomb was cursed just a few days after it was opened. Carter's canary was killed by a cobra. Cobras were believed to protect the pharaohs. A few months later, Lord George Carnarvon, who paid for the expedition, died from blood poisoning. A month after that, a visitor to the tomb died from a fever and another was shot dead by his wife. The person who X-rayed the mummy found in the tomb died mysteriously. By 1932, 6 people connected with the tomb were dead, and Carter himself died of cancer in 1939.

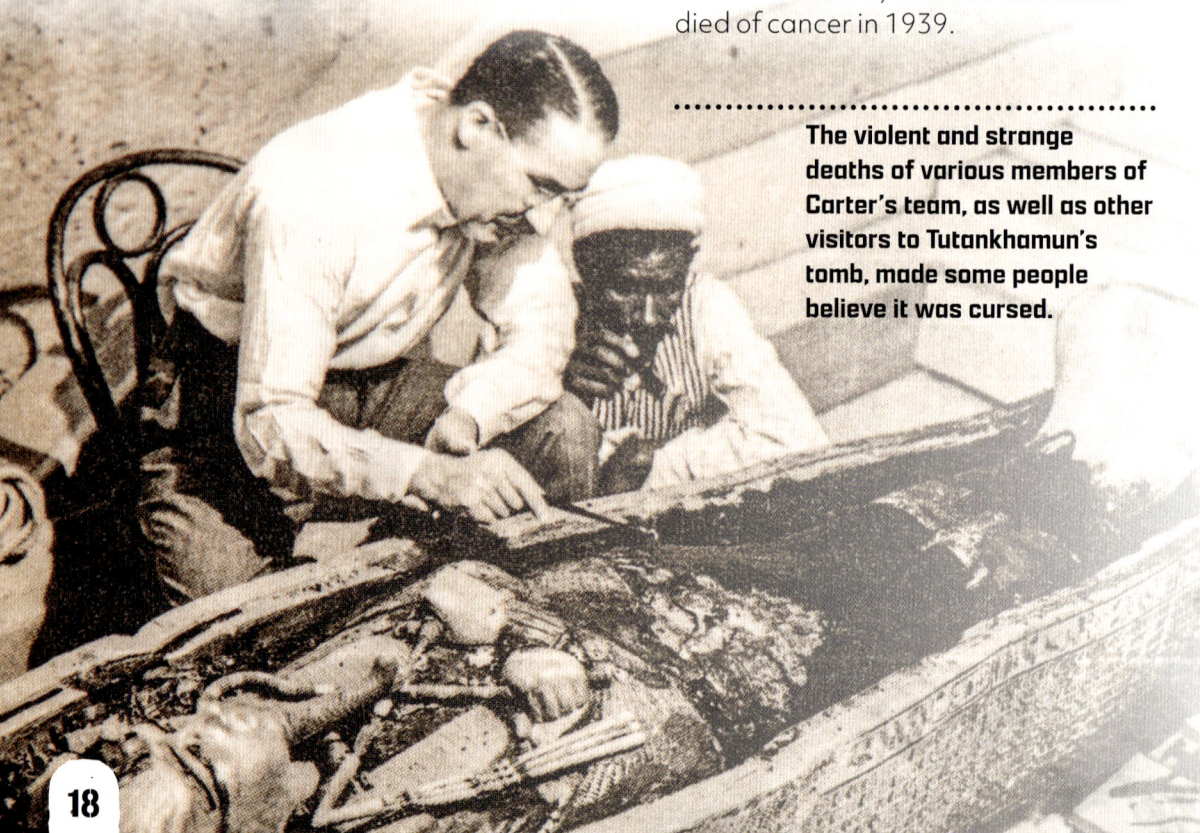

The violent and strange deaths of various members of Carter's team, as well as other visitors to Tutankhamun's tomb, made some people believe it was cursed.

A Cursed Tomb?

Was Tutankhamun's tomb really cursed? At the moment of Lord Carnarvon's death, it was said that all the lights went out in Cairo, which was really spooky! Yet, most people believe that this and the deaths were just coincidences. In the past, it was not as easy to treat illnesses such as blood poisoning and fever as it is today. There were no vaccinations for travelers, so it wasn't unusual for them to get sick. Was Tut's tomb cursed, or were the deaths and illnesses simply strange coincidences?

A Mask of Death

One of the most amazing finds in the tomb was Tutankhamun's death mask. Death masks were made to look like the dead person and they were supposed to help the pharaoh's soul recognize its body, so that it could return to it in the afterlife. Death masks were also believed to protect a dead person from evil spirits in the afterlife.

....

For the richest and most important Egyptians, the death mask would have been made of gold. Tutankhamun's death mask was made from two layers of gold and covered with beautiful gems.

CHAPTER 3
DEADLY TOMBS

In ancient times in China and Mongolia, Asia, the tombs of powerful leaders were elaborate—and deadly. Some were dug very deep below the surface of the earth and the coffins containing the dead were hidden there. A coffin was usually surrounded by gold, silver, bronze, and **jade** treasures, clothing, and food. More spookily, some tombs also contained the bodies of animals and people. The people were relatives of the dead ruler, or his servants and slaves. They were killed and buried with their leader so they could serve them in the afterlife.

Buried Secretly

Ancient leaders often spent a large part of their lives planning their tombs. Their afterlife and what they would take with them were hugely important. They spent a fortune on their tombs and their contents to ensure their afterlife journey was similar to their life in this world. The tombs were not only deep underground, but also in secret locations to protect them from tomb raiders. Many such tombs also contained traps or deadly devices to stop or harm anyone who dared to enter.

There are reports of ancient Chinese tombs containing poisonous gases and deadly weapons designed to kill any intruder.

SPOOKED!

Evidence suggests that many of the people buried alongside emperors in ancient China were not killed in a **sacrificial** ritual before the tomb was closed. Instead they were buried alive!

Thankfully, in later times in ancient China, figures of people were buried with emperors, rather than real and living people!

Secret Schemes

Some ancient rulers went to great lengths to ensure no one knew where they were buried. Tu Dúc ruled an **empire** in Vietnam from 1848 to 1883. He built a burial site and tomb in the capital city of his empire. There was a grand tomb monument, a large lake, and nearly 50 buildings. Everyone believed that when Tu Dúc died, he would have a grand royal burial there. But the scheming ruler had other plans…

Silenced Forever

Tu Dúc had been building a second burial site all along. To make sure no one could tell where it was, he ordered that all the workers who buried him were murdered after their work was complete. Their heads were cut off to ensure their silence! The emperor's burial site remains a mystery to this day.

A Tomb of Weapons and Magic

When China's Emperor Liu Fei died, he was buried in an elaborate tomb that lay hidden for more than 2,000 years. When archeologists finally opened the tomb in 2014, they found 3 major tombs, 11 smaller ones, 2 pits full of spearheads and knives, and some other weapons.

They also found pits that contained **chariots** and horses' skeletons. There was a kitchen and food, many objects made from gold, silver, and gemstones, and more than 100,000 coins: everything the spoiled king would need for the afterlife.

A Jade Coffin

Liu Fei's body was missing. It was probably stolen long ago. But, in his tomb were pieces of jade, and in another tomb, an entire coffin made of jade. In ancient China, jade was a precious and rare stone. It was a symbol of power. Jade was also believed to have magical powers and could keep away bad spirits. Important Chinese leaders were often buried in jade armor.

Jade burial suits were thought to be magical and allowed the person wearing them to live forever.

SPOOKED!

The 11 smaller tombs were found to the north of the emperor's tomb. Could these have been for people killed when he died? Experts think human sacrifice had stopped in China by this time, but they are not sure.

Genghis Khan was a mighty and respected leader. His army was determined to keep his burial place a secret, and killed anyone who could reveal its whereabouts.

A Tomb of Doom

Genghis Khan ruled a mighty empire that stretched from China in the east all the way to eastern Europe. When Genghis Khan died, his army obeyed his order to bury him in secret. As they carried his body to its final resting place, they killed anyone unlucky enough to meet them on their way. They also killed the slaves who built his underground tomb. After the army had buried the emperor, they rode 1,000 horses over the burial site to cover any signs that something had been buried there. Then the soldiers killed themselves.

A Cursed Burial Place?

Genghis Khan died in 1227 and since his death, no one has found his tomb. There are several theories about where in Mongolia the grave may be. Some believe it's likely to be full of precious objects, horses, and people to keep him company. There is one place it might be: a holy mountain protected by the Mongolians. But no outsiders are allowed to go there. Many Mongolians believe that anyone who disturbs a grave will be cursed. So, perhaps we will never know.

INVESTIGATING QIN'S BURIAL SITE

Streams of Death

Archeologists have found the tomb of Qin, the first emperor of China, but they dare not enter it! There are reports that builders of the tomb were told to make traps that would fire arrows at anyone trying to enter. Archeologists have also discovered rivers of the poisonous liquid metal mercury running around the tomb. As well as these streams of death, it is likely that there are more traps waiting to target any intruders.

The Magic of Mercury

Qin became more and more interested in magic as he aged. He wanted to find a magical potion that would help him live forever. He even drank mercury because he thought it might make him immortal, or able to live forever. In reality, the deadly mercury probably killed the ruler!

Buried Alive!

Qin's body is not the only one buried at the site. There are burial pits around the main tomb containing the remains of female servants, killed to follow and serve their leader in his afterlife. Qin also ordered that all the builders who made his tomb be killed, for fear that they might reveal the secrets of its contents. After the funeral, the gates were closed and the builders were buried alive, sealed inside the tomb to die alongside their emperor. It took 720,000 people to build the tomb complex. How many of them died there?

An Empire for the Afterlife

In his tomb complex, Qin was trying to recreate his earthly empire for the next world. His main tomb is said to contain hoards of rare treasures and a ceiling made to look like the night sky, with pearls for stars. The mercury was used to recreate China's rivers. In pits around the main tomb were figures of dancers, acrobats, and strongmen for the emperor's entertainment. They were made from the brownish-orange stone called terracotta.

Army of the Dead?

Guarding Qin's empire for the afterlife are 8,000 clay soldiers. It is called the Terracotta Army. Each figure is unique, with different details on their faces, uniforms, and hair. The terracotta soldiers face away from the emperor's tomb. They were positioned to protect the emperor and his tomb. In other burial pits, there are statues of horses, bronze carriages, and even a magnificent chariot. This was everything an army might need in war.

Was the emperor, who fought many wars in life, preparing for battle in the afterlife?

CHAPTER 4

TREASURE-FILLED TOMBS

Tombs filled with treasure can be found below temples and palaces deep in the tangled rain forests of Central and South America. The kings buried within them were believed to become gods after they died. They were buried with jade, gold, and other riches to prove that they were important, so the gods would accept them as one of their own. Kings' tombs were also filled with lavish burial gifts for them to use in the afterlife. Alongside these riches, there was often something more gruesome: the remains of human or animal sacrifices.

Blood Offerings

Offerings of blood were made by ancient people such as the Maya to nourish their gods. Sometimes, this was done by **bloodletting**. A king would cut his skin and let the blood drop into a bowl. Sacrifice was the most important type of bloodletting. Animals such as turkeys, dogs, squirrels, and lizards were sacrificed on top of large pyramids that were built as temples. The most important Mayan rituals, such as the funeral of kings, included human sacrifice. Usually, prisoners of war and slaves were killed in sacrifice. The victims' heads were cut off or their hearts were removed. It was gruesome!

The Maya performed scary ceremonies and carried out horrible sacrifices on top of their temples.

Journey to the Underworld

Ancient **Mesoamerican** people believed that the dead went first to a place full of demons called the Underworld. If they survived this, they could go to Heaven. The faces of dead kings and queens were often covered in death masks. A death mask was meant to protect the wearer on their dreadful journey. The masks were often made from jade, one of the most precious gems, and looked a lot like their owners.

Life in Death

Families used to leave food offerings for their loved ones to use on their journey to the Underworld and to eat in the next life. They believed that making regular offerings to their ancestors meant the dead would watch over the living and keep them safe. Another sign of respect was even creepier—they dug up the bodies of the dead, cleaned the bones, and reburied the bodies. Sometimes, they kept the skulls and decorated them as a sign of respect.

The Maya often killed enemies their fearsome warriors captured in battle by sacrificing them.

SPOOKED!

Mesoamericans were used to seeing hundreds or thousands of skulls in their plazas, or city centers. Huge racks stacked with human skulls were often put out for public display!

The Red Queen

The Red Queen was found in a sealed stone sarcophagus full of gems in Palenque, a Mayan city in southern Mexico. The queen earned her nickname because after she had been placed in the sarcophagus, her body was covered with a thick layer of blood-red cinnabar. This toxic powder stained the sarcophagus and the Queen's bones. The cinnabar covering her can release fumes that are toxic if breathed in! As her flesh rotted away, it left a shockingly red skeleton on view.

Companions in Death

The Red Queen went to the afterlife with two companions. One was a young boy of around 10 years old who had been sacrificed by beheading, and there was also an adult woman whose heart had been taken out. She had also been stabbed and her blood removed. It is likely that her blood and heart were offered to the gods.

A Death Mask

The queen was also found wearing an eerie death mask made from 280 pieces of a precious green stone called malachite. Inside the sarcophagus was a treasure trove of more than 1,000 pieces of precious stone.

This is the death mask of the Red Queen. The mask has black stone eyes that seem to look directly at you!

Death Within the Devil's Pyramid

El Diablo, or the Devil's pyramid-temple, lies in the Mayan city of El Zotz in Guatemala in Central America. **Looters** had begun to dig a deep trench there in search of treasure. This trench led archeologists to a series of gruesome finds, not far below where the looters had given up and stopped digging. Their finds included blood-red bowls filled with human fingers, bejeweled teeth, and the remains of children.

A Stench of Decay

Below these spooky finds was a tomb. When archeologists opened it, they were hit by a powerful stench of decay and a chill in the air. Inside the tomb were the remains of a king named Chak and a large number of ceramics, textiles, and other rich offerings. Arranged around Chak were the skulls and other remains of six children. They were probably killed in sacrifice and placed in the tomb as offerings to the dead man.

SPOOKED!

Young adults were often sacrificed during the burial of Mayan kings. But it was more unusual to sacrifice very young children. The spine-chilling remains at El Zotz included bones belonging to children as young as 12 months old!

Archeologists are used to unearthing the bones of ancient people, but it must be shocking for those who discovered the remains of the children at El Zotz.

Follow the Avenue of Death

In the ancient Aztec city of Teotihuacan in Mexico, you can follow in the footsteps of a person who was sacrificed, if you are brave enough! To do so, you would walk down Avenue of the Dead to the Pyramid of the Moon. Then, you'd take the staircase to a stage where grisly sacrifices of animals and humans were performed. It was also a tomb for the poor victims of these gruesome rituals.

Tombs of Terror

One burial chamber contained the remains of 12 victims of sacrifice—10 of them had been beheaded. The spooky room also contained other offerings and the remains of various animals. In another chamber were the remains of a man who had been tied up and sacrificed. He was surrounded by more than 150 burial offerings, including mirrors, shells, and the remains of 8 hawks or falcons, and 2 jaguars. The animals were most likely buried alive.

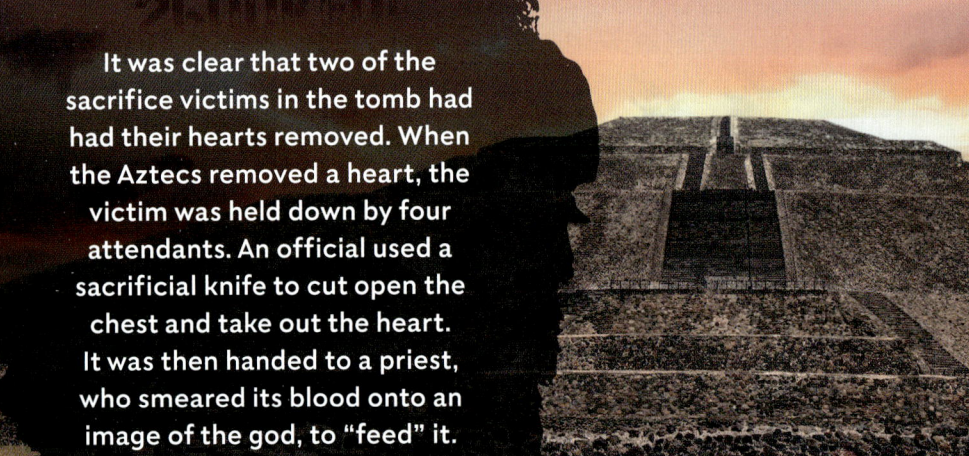

SPOOKED!

It was clear that two of the sacrifice victims in the tomb had had their hearts removed. When the Aztecs removed a heart, the victim was held down by four attendants. An official used a sacrificial knife to cut open the chest and take out the heart. It was then handed to a priest, who smeared its blood onto an image of the god, to "feed" it. Then the body was thrown down the pyramid steps.

Would you walk up the stairs at the Pyramid of the Moon in Teotihuacan?

Archeologists have the gruesome job of studying victims' remains found in tombs to learn how they died.

A Golden Chief

In 2011, archeologists found a 1,000-year-old tomb in Panama, Central America, filled with treasures and evidence of a strange and unusual method of murder. The tomb was the final resting place of an important leader of an ancient people known as the Golden Warriors. The skeleton of the Golden chief lay on a platform. He was surrounded by the remains of 15 bodies. These bodies were carefully placed around the leader. They were most likely prisoners of war or slaves who were sacrificed or killed themselves.

Death by Pufferfish?

The archeologists uncovered a creepy clue as to how the sacrificed people died. Near the bodies there was a container filled with the bones of a pufferfish. This is a very poisonous fish and would have caused extreme pain. The pain would have started with a tingling sensation in the fingers. The poisoned person would remain fully aware of what was happening to them, but they soon wouldn't have been able to move any parts of their body, sit up, or speak. It could take minutes or, at worse, even up to six hours before they stopped breathing and died.

INVESTIGATING MISSING INCA GOLD

Braving the Forests

Somewhere deep inside the misty Llanganates mountain range in Ecuador, South America, there is an extraordinary hoard of ancient Inca treasure. At least that is what treasure seekers who brave this scary place with its dense tangled forests, treacherous lakes and rivers, and muddy swamps believe. For more than 500 years, treasure hunters have risked the difficult conditions there, hoping that they will be the ones to finally find the legendary Inca treasure.

Lost Inca Gold

The Inca controlled a huge empire in western South America from the middle of the fifteenth century. They mined large amounts of gold and silver, and used it to make jewelry and ornaments, and to decorate their palaces. Inca temples, monuments, roads, and gardens all glittered with gold. Some objects were even made of solid gold. One famous emperor named Atahualpa is said to have sat on a throne of pure gold.

An Emperor in Trouble

Atahualpa was in charge when Spanish invaders, known as conquistadors, arrived in 1532. The Spanish took Atahualpa prisoner. The emperor offered the Spanish a vast amount of gold, enough to fill a whole room, in return for his freedom.

Revenge for Murder

The legend says that an Inca general in charge of 60,000 men was bringing an enormous amount of gold for the conquistadors when he found out that they had murdered Atahualpa. The furious general sent his men to hide the treasure. We don't know if it was buried deep underground, hidden in a deep cave, or dropped into a lake. The Spanish captured and tortured the general but the brave soldier never revealed the treasure's location.

A Cursed Treasure?

The search for the Inca gold has haunted treasure hunters ever since. About 50 years after Atahualpa's death, a Spanish man named Valverde claimed he found the treasure. He left directions to its location before he died. The leader of one team that followed these clues mysteriously vanished. Stories of curses and danger put off many others. In 1886, two men who found the treasure died on their way home. In 1912, an American treasure hunter's wife died after their camp was swept away by floods, and he went insane shortly afterward. It seemed that all had been cursed…

A Tragic Fate?

An American man who went in search of the gold in the late 1990s suffered a strange and tragic fate. He was an experienced traveler but he suddenly tripped, slipped, and fell down a mountain slope and fell onto a broken tree trunk, and died.

Many people have tried and failed to find the lost Inca treasure and some have lost their lives chasing this legendary fortune.

The Spanish conquistadors were determined to find the Inca gold.

CHAPTER 5

SWALLOWED BY THE SEA

Stories of treasure-filled ships that have been swallowed by the sea have fascinated people for centuries. Many unfortunate treasure hunters have died searching for the lost ships scattered across the world's ocean floors. Some of these ships were sunk after being attacked by pirates or enemies. Others met their doom after being caught in wild waves or violent storms. When ships end up on the bottom of the ocean, the darkness, the depth, and the freezing temperatures there make it very dangerous for anyone who tries to find them. Despite that, many still try.

Stealing Treasures

Why were ancient ships carrying **cargoes** of gold and other amazing treasures? From the fifteenth to the early twentieth centuries, the leaders of some countries sent ships to explore the world and to bring back any riches they found on their travels. Spanish ships sailed to South and Central America and brought back Aztec and Inca gold, for example. But, many of these ships were lost on their way home. Some were victims of foul weather. Others were robbed and destroyed by the crews of other ships, who got to know the routes these treasure ships would take, and lay in wait to **ambush** them at sea.

Unimaginable Fortune

For nearly 250 years, treasure chests filled with gold, silver, and emeralds lay hidden alongside the skeletons of the sailors who went to the bottom of the sea with them. Then in 1985, the 250-year-old Spanish galleon (a sailing ship) *Nuestra Señora de Atocha* was discovered off the Florida coast. Its treasure is worth $450 million, making it the most valuable shipwreck ever found.

SPOOKED!

The search for the *Atocha* was long and dangerous. Three people lost their lives during this quest after their treasure-hunting boat capsized, or overturned, just days after their discovery of some of the *Atocha* cannons.

34

Long ago, carrying valuable goods across the ocean was the only way to transport the riches over great distances.

Drowned at Sea

In 1622, the *Nuestra Señora de Atocha* was sailing from the Americas to Spain when it was hit by a hurricane and started to sink. Only five people—three sailors and two slaves—survived by climbing the mast, which poked out above the water. Their rescuers tried to get into the ship but the hatches were tightly locked. Then a second hurricane scattered the remains of the *Atocha* so widely, it seemed the ship had vanished altogether. A total of 260 people lost their lives in the disaster.

The vast treasure found in the shipwreck of the *Nuestra Señora de las Mercedes*, seen exploding in the center of this painting, weighed 17 tons (15.4 mt).

Sunken Riches

In 1804, the *Nuestra Señora de las Mercedes* sank off the coast of Portugal on its way from Montevideo in Uraquay to Cádiz in Spain. At the time, the warship was carrying a hoard of treasure, which was reportedly worth as much as $500 million, from Spanish **colonies** in lands in South America to Spain.

Explosion on Board

When a squadron of British naval ships attacked the *Nuestra Señora de las Mercedes*, it exploded and spilled all of its contents, including its treasure. Hundreds of Spanish naval officers, crew, and civilians, or ordinary people, met their death when the ship sank. The remaining 50 crewmen were taken prisoner by the British.

Treasure in the Deep

In the years after the *Nuestra Señora de las Mercedes* sank, underwater animals ate away the wood on the ship and salt water wore away the metal. But the ship still clung tightly onto its treasures because gold and silver do not corrode, and almost 600,000 silver coins and more than 200 gold coins have been found. The beautiful metals were mined and the coins made in the Andes, from places that are now in Bolivia, Chile, and Peru.

Lost at Sea

In 1708, the *San José* was traveling to Colombia, carrying treasures collected from Spanish colonies, when an English ship attacked it for its treasure. The *San José* sank so suddenly and quickly that nearly all 600 crewmen aboard at the time were lost with the ship. The entire fortune in gold, silver, emeralds, and other jewels was lost to the deep and to both the Spanish and the English who had fought over it.

Gone Forever?

For centuries, treasure seekers, explorers, and archeologists dreamed of finding the sunken shipwreck and its riches. However, the ship lay 3,000 feet (914 m) under the water. It was impossible to locate until new technology in the form of robotic submarines made it possible to explore, find, and photograph the ship in 2015. It was found lying on its side near the island of Baru off the coast of Colombia. Piles of gold coins and trinkets lie scattered on the ocean floor around the *San José*. The treasure remains there because Spain, Colombia, the explorers, and the people from whom the treasure was stolen continue to argue about who owns it.

The promise of finding treasure drives some divers to explore dangerous wrecks deep beneath the waves.

SPOOKED!

As the *San José* sank, the crew were trapped inside the ship. They sank to the ocean floor and the shipwreck became their tomb.

INVESTIGATING A SLAVE SHIP

Pirates Ahoy!

The *Whydah Gally* has a dark and sinister history. It was built as a slave ship in 1715, to transport slaves from Africa to the Caribbean. But while it was returning from Jamaica, the **notorious** pirate "Black Sam" Bellamy **hijacked** it. Black Sam and his crew took over the *Whydah Gally* and used it to attack and steal from many other unfortunate ships. The ship was fast and equipped with 28 cannons, and in command of it, Bellamy became a very wealthy pirate.

Pirate Plunder

Then on a dark and stormy night in April 1717, the ship went down somewhere off the coast of Cape Cod. Strong winds were whipping up high, rough waves. The *Whydah Gally* slammed into a sandbar, capsized, and broke apart. Wreckage from the ship was quickly swallowed up by the shifting sands in the area. At the time, the pirate ship was rumored to be carrying the treasure stolen from 53 other ships, divided equally among the pirates and stored in their own personal treasure chests on board the vessel.

One of Bellamy's crew bragged that they raised a large black flag, featuring a skull and crossed bones, when they chased their victims.

One of the pirates died holding a pistol in his hand and gold stashed in his pocket.

Skeletons in the Shipwreck

Only two of the 146 crewmen on the *Whydah Gally* survived. The bodies of 101 crewmen eventually washed up on the beach, but 43 went down with the ship. Archeologists have found six skeletons in the shipwreck, some with bones that were probably broken when the ship capsized.

Untold Treasures

The shipwreck hid its secrets for more than 260 years, mystifying hopeful treasure seekers. Then in 1984, the wreck was finally discovered under deep layers of sand. Bellamy was only 28 years old when the *Whydah Gally* went down but he had already had a successful career as a pirate. More than 200,000 artifacts, or items from the past, were recovered from the wreck, including 15,000 coins, gems, pistols, and other weapons.

A Pleasant Pirate?

Black Sam was named for his long, black hair. His crew was made up of African slaves, perhaps freed from the slave ship, Native Americans, and sailors from across Europe and North America. Bellamy was said to treat all his crew equally and let them all vote on important decisions. There is no record of him ever killing a captive, and he often returned captured ships and cargo if they were no use to him.

CHAPTER 6
TREASURE HUNTERS IN ACTION

There is still treasure out there waiting for treasure hunters to find it. There could be more than a million undiscovered shipwrecks still submerged underwater. There is buried treasure too. Some treasure was taken by cruel and deadly means and lost the same way. Finding such cursed riches is difficult, challenging, and sometimes, deadly.

Captain Kidd's Treasure

Captain Kidd was one of the most famous pirates of all time. It is said that his enormous stash of treasure would be worth more than $15 million in today's money. Kidd was arrested for piracy and murder in Britain in 1699. He had jewels on his ship at that time but the rest of his treasure was never found. What happened to his fortune has remained a mystery, though treasure hunters believe he buried it somewhere on his travels.

Billions Lost in Battles

Some treasure hoards were collected and lost during the deadliest wars. At the end of the Civil War in the United States in 1865, the defeated Confederate side escaped with millions of dollars worth of gold. Legend has it that the soldiers hid it so that their opponents would never find it. During World War II (1939–1945), the Nazi Germans hid vast amounts of money and treasures they had looted in Europe. In 2023, an old map was unearthed that seemed to reveal where German soldiers buried diamonds, rubies, gold, and silver in the Netherlands. However, nothing has been found, yet...

The Kruger Millions

The Boer War (1899–1902) was fought in South Africa between the British and the Boers, who were **descendants** of Dutch people who settled there. The Boer president Paul Kruger escaped with a stash of gold bars and coins worth more than $5 billion today. But, the train that was carrying the treasure mysteriously vanished on its way to Mozambique, a country that borders South Africa. Since then, many treasure hunters have tried to find Kruger's millions but searches have failed.

Captain Kidd's first job was hunting pirates, before he himself became a criminal. Then, he too was a wanted man and was on the run.

SPOOKED!

When Kidd was being executed for piracy in 1701, the hangman's rope broke. He fell to the ground and was still alive. But he was not let off. Kidd was forced to climb up the steps of the gallows for a second time. When he was hanged again, the rope did not break.

Deadly Treasure Hunts

Treasure hunting can be dangerous! In 2010, an art collector named Forrest Fenn buried a treasure chest of rare and valuable objects worth $1 million in the Rocky Mountains. He hid clues to its secret location in a map and a mysterious poem at the end of a book he wrote called *The Thrill of the Chase*. Searchers began looking for the treasure immediately. At one point it was said that up to 2 million people were looking for the stash.

Risks and Rewards

The Rocky Mountains are a wild and forbidding place and some treasure hunters put themselves at great personal risk. At least five men are known to have died while hunting for Fenn's treasure. Some treasure hunters spent their life savings or quit their jobs to find the chest. Some broke into Fenn's home in an attempt to find more clues. The treasure was finally found in June 2020. Fenn himself died three months later.

SPOOKED!

The five people who died trying to find Fenn's treasure chest lost their lives by falling down crevices, losing control of rafts, or from terrible weather conditions.

Greed for Gold

In the early 1930s, there was an **economic crisis**. Gold often rises in value during such times because it is a safe investment. A millionaire named Leon Trabuco and his partners bought a lot of gold in Mexico and smuggled it into the United States, where they hoped to sell it for a large profit. Then, the US government changed the law, making it impossible for Trabuco to sell his gold. So Trabuco hid it.

Bad Luck or Cursed?

The treasure brought nothing but bad luck. Within five years, three of Trabuco's partners had mysteriously died. Trabuco never revealed the gold's location or made a map. He took its secret location to the grave. One treasure hunter who thought he found the gold after decades looking for it, died before he could dig it up! Some say Trabuco's gold was found long ago by the US government. Others say that it is still hidden somewhere in the harsh New Mexico desert.

Treasure Hunters Beware!

Have you ever felt the urge to grab a map and spade, and go digging for gold or other treasure? Stories of lost tombs and treasures often tempt people, but they should take care. The curses that are often linked with hidden treasure may not be real but the risks of hunting for riches in far-off places or deep oceans most certainly are! Many treasure hunters have been hurt or killed chasing secret stashes of gold and gems. Perhaps, after all, treasure is best left buried!

One man who searched for Fenn's treasure was caught digging up graves in an attempt to find it!

INVESTIGATING THE KNIGHTS

Famous Knights

The Knights Templar was one of the most famous groups of knights of the **Middle Ages**. They were known not only for their deadly fighting skills on the battlefield but also for the wealth they gathered during the Crusades. The Crusades were military expeditions taken on by European Christians. The Crusaders believed they were doing their God's work by fighting to "reclaim" the city of Jerusalem for Christianity from the Muslims who then ruled it. Like many others who went on the Crusades, the Knights Templar also wanted money and power!

Getting Rich

Jerusalem is important to Christians because it is the place where they believe Jesus died and was buried. Christians have visited the city for centuries. The Knights Templar set up headquarters, or their main office, there. They were declared a charity by the pope, the head of the Catholic Church. To help them in their work, wealthy Christians in Europe gave the Knights Templar gifts of gold, silver, jewels, land, castles, and fighting men for 170 years. Unlike almost everyone else, the knights were not asked to pay taxes or money to the Church.

Arrested and Escaped

In the 1300s, the Muslims regained control of Jerusalem, from where they believe the Prophet Muhammad ascended, or rose, to Heaven. The knights were arrested in France and accused of failing the Church. Some top-ranking knights were burned to death as punishment. Many knights escaped. It is believed they took their vast treasures and priceless objects with them to hide somewhere. The question is, where did they take it?

A Money Pit

There are many theories about what happened to the treasure. One is that the knights took their treasures by ship to Oak Island, off the coast of Nova Scotia in Canada. Treasure hunters have discovered a deep pit where they think the Knights Templar treasure may lie. The trouble is, it is thought the knights built flood traps to prevent anyone reaching the treasure at the bottom. When people try to dig deep into the pit, this treacherous hole floods with water. Several people have been hurt or died in the spooky money pit.

Templars Today

Some people believe that there is a top-secret group of Knights Templar working together today and that they know where the treasure was buried!

The Knights Templar gradually became one of the richest organizations of their time.

GLOSSARY

ambush to attack by surprise from a hidden place
bacteria tiny living things, some of which can cause disease
bloodletting the act of letting blood by opening a vein
burial sites places where dead people are laid to rest or buried
cargoes goods carried by ship, truck, or other vehicle
chariots two-wheeled vehicles drawn by horses
colonies groups of people who settle in a new place
complex a group of buildings
cultures a particular group of people with a particular way of life
descendants people who are related to someone who lived long ago
economic crisis a time when there are great concerns about money
empire a group of countries or regions that are controlled by one ruler or one government
expedition an organized journey for a particular purpose
fungi group of living things that includes yeast and mushrooms
gallows a wooden structure used to hang criminals
hieroglyphs pictures or symbols that represent words, parts of words, or sounds
hijacked taken illegally
jade a green precious stone
lapis-lazuli a blue precious stone
legends traditional stories
looters people who steal during a war or riot
marsh an area of low, flat land that is usually covered in shallow water
Mesoamerican a historical region from the southern part of North America to most of Central America
Middle Ages the period between the end of the Roman Empire lasting from CE 476 to about CE 1500
Norse belonging or relating to Scandinavian countries
notorious famous for something bad
quicksand deep, wet sand that sucks in anyone who tries to walk across it
rituals actions performed in a certain way, especially as part of a religious ceremony
sacred holy, or connected with the gods
sacrificial describes something killed to honor a god or gods
Soviet Union a powerful country made up of 15 states, the largest of which was Russia, which existed from 1922 to 1991
trade buy and sell goods and services
tyrannous describes someone who uses their power cruelly

FIND OUT MORE

Books

Deary, Terry. *All at Sea* (Horrible Histories). Scholastic, 2022.

Enz, Tammy. *Science in King Tut's Tomb* (Science of History). Capstone Press, 2021.

Fleming, Candace. *The Curse of the Mummy: Uncovering Tutankhamun's Tomb* (True Stories in Focus). Scholastic, 2021.

Long, David. *Amazing Treasures: 100+ Objects and Places That Will Boggle Your Mind* (Our Amazing World, 2). What on Earth Books, 2021.

Websites

Read more about Tutankhamun's tomb at:
https://kids.nationalgeographic.com/history/article/the-discovery-of-king-tuts-tomb

Learn more about pirates at:
https://www.dkfindout.com/uk/history/pirates

There's more treasure to be found at:
https://online.kidsdiscover.com/unit/buried-treasure

Publisher's note to educators and parents:
All the websites featured above have been carefully reviewed to ensure that they are suitable for students. However, many websites change often, and we cannot guarantee that a site's future contents will continue to meet our high standards of educational value. Please be advised that students should be closely monitored whenever they access the Internet.

INDEX

Africa 16–19, 38, 39, 40
afterlife 4, 12–13, 16, 19, 20, 22, 24, 26, 27, 28
ancient China 20–25
ancient Egypt 12–19
archeologists 8, 10, 11, 15, 16, 17, 18, 22, 24, 29, 31, 37, 39
Asia 8–9, 10–11, 20–25
Aztec 30, 34

burial sites 4, 17, 21, 22, 23, 24–25, 30 (*see also* tombs)

Cleopatra 14–15
curses 4, 5, 10–11, 13, 15, 18–19, 23, 32–33, 40, 43

death masks 5, 19, 27, 28
deserts 4, 43

El Dorado 6
Europe 6–7, 8, 11, 23, 35, 36, 37, 39, 40, 44

Genghis Khan 23

hoax 8

Inca 32–33, 34

Kingdom of Saguenay 6–7

legends/stories 4, 6, 7, 8, 13, 32–33, 34, 40, 43
Liu Fei 22

Maya 26–29
Middle Ages 44

North America 6–7, 26–31, 34, 35, 38–39, 40, 42, 43, 44

oceans 4, 5, 34–39, 43

pirates 4, 5, 34, 38–39, 40–41

Qin 24–25

sacrifice 21, 22, 26, 27, 28, 29, 30, 31
shipwrecks 5, 34–35, 36, 37, 38–39
South America 6, 26, 32–33, 34, 36, 37

Timur the Great 10–11
tombs 4, 5, 10–11, 12–19, 20–25, 26–31, 37, 43
treasure 4–9, 12–19, 20, 22, 24, 26–33, 34–39, 40–45
treasure hunters 4–11, 32–33, 34, 37, 39, 40–45
Tu Dúc 21
Tutankhamun 18–19

About the Author
Louise Spilsbury is an award-winning children's book author. She has written countless books about history and science. In writing and researching this book, she is more spooked than ever by cursed tombs and treasure.